1913 Flood in Defiance, Ohio

Trish Sanford-Speiser

Dedicated to those who continually decide to help.

To my DEAR Friends
Linda + Phil

Riverview Press
Defiance, Ohio

Printed in the United States of America
by The Hubbard Company, Defiance, Ohio 43512

Cover Photo by Ed Bronson. Taken from the court house steps facing west. Rod Brown Photo Collection.

Right Photo - Photographer, Ed Bronson's camera is looking north on Clinton Street. Corner of Clinton and First Street. Newly built Masonic Temple seen to right. Rod Brown Photo Collection.

The Maumee & Auglaize

Rivers of Power & Force

The Maumee River alone drains about 6,000 square miles of land across Northeast Indiana and Northwest Ohio sending its waters on to Lake Erie. It was dug thousands of years ago by the receding glacier that once covered the tri-state area. In downtown Defiance, the Maumee River meets the terminus of the Auglaize River draining lands from the south. The combined Maumee & Auglaize is the largest tributary to Lake Erie, moving an immense volume of water each day.

This water power was harnessed by the early pioneers in various and innovative ways. Early settlers built sawmills and grain-mills which sourced their power from the moving waters that turned their machines and powered their belts to drive the blades and stones that cut and ground the land's raw materials into wood boards and nourishing grains, building and sustaining life in this new and untamed land. The rivers were later channeled into hand dug trenches called canals which moved people and goods between the civilized East and the frontier West throughout the 1800s. In downtown Defiance, factories of every sort sprung up along the canal and built millraces along the powerful waters to drive their manufacturing.

Eventually, a central fire station was built in the midst of Defiance's commercial district offering protection from industry's greatest hazard: fire. Pumps were installed, and hydrants were built that could push water through hoses and suppress the hungry flames. Towers were built throughout the area, manned with lookouts watching for any wisp of smoke or sign of flame. In 1888 innovators figured out a way to build a "stand pipe" measuring 140 feet tall and 22 feet in diameter pumped full of water from the river. Simple gravity driven pressure pushed the water through a maze of pipes that gradually supplied the city with muddy running water.

Defiance further tamed the rivers with seven bridges, working from the west toward the Auglaize: the state owned "Mule Bridge" for the canal, then the "Wabash Railroad Bridge," and the Clinton Street Bridge; all spanning the Maumee River. Crossing the Auglaize River was the Second Street Bridge, the Hopkins Street Bridge, the B&O Railroad Bridge, and at the end of what is now Riverside Avenue, the Francis Street Bridge. Spring flooding always brought hazards and damage to Defiance's water dependent businesses; the power of the water offered risk as well as reward. But never had the people seen the destruction that began Easter Sunday in March of 1913 when it began to rain.

Maumee River and Water-Works Tower, Defiance, O.

Postcard of the Defiance Public Waterworks on the Banks of the Maumee. Jo McCormick Collection

Easter Sunday

March 23, 1913

Ohio had just reached its 110th year of statehood, when on Easter Sunday of 1913, it began to rain. Storm clouds seemed to hover across the entire Midwest. It had already been a very wet winter leaving the ground completely saturated with spring rains. Hearty citizens probably thought it was just another rainy day. Little did they know, Ohio was about to experience the largest natural disaster it had ever seen. The damage from the 1913 Flood is unsurpassed to this day.

The whole affair really started up with an ominous wind storm on Friday night which damaged a good portion of the roof on the East Defiance Citizen's Band clubhouse saturating the building's interior

"It 'aint no use to grumble and Complain. It's just as easy to rejoice, When God sorts out the weather And sends rain, Why, rain's my choice."

– Director W. F. Kimberly

Left photo offered by Jo McCormick, Albert Diehl and James Hamilton Private Collection.

Right photo, from Barbara Warncke, granddaughter of W. Kimberly.

when the rains started up on Sunday. The band was out and about on that Easter morning playing for the residents of Defiance's east side. The band members returned to their quarters that afternoon to find it in a horrible state.

To make matters worse, the members of the band had just finished a four year fundraising and renovation job making themselves a proper clubhouse at 619 Ottawa Avenue complete with a rehearsal hall, a reading room and piano. Monday's Crescent-News went on to report the members of the club remained throughly optimistic despite the crumbling plaster, ruined wallpaper and soaked furnishings.

Director W. F. Kimberly was quoted on the front page of that Monday paper as follows:

"It 'aint no use to grumble and Complain. It's just as easy to rejoice, When God sorts out the weather And sends rain, Why, rain's my choice."

One wonders if Mr. Kimberly ever lived down those words given the disaster that ensued.

W. F. KIMBERLY
Director

Tuesday

March 25, 1913

It had not stopped raining since Easter Sunday. It was raining in Fort Wayne too. Defiance received a message from the weather observer there simply reading "Floods Unprecedented". Fort Wayne was at 25 feet flood stage at 1:30 this Tuesday afternoon and Defiance was preparing to reach 22 feet sometime in the night.

There was no mail delivery to Defiance on Tuesday as the water had cut off the railroad between Defiance and Fort Wayne. At 10:30 this morning there was 9 feet of water going over the newly built Power Dam out on the Auglaize River, and it was rising four inches each hour.

The pumps at the city waterworks were operated by steam engines. Water was heated with fire, which created steam pressure and drove the pumps forcing water into its massive standpipe holding thousands of gallons of water. The fires that fed those pumps at the Wabash Pumping Station were overwhelmed with floodwaters by noon on Tuesday shutting down the water plant and causing the entire town to lose water pressure.

The back of the Defiance Creamery, on the south side of the Maumee beside the Clinton Street bridge, crumbled from the water. The water was in the basements of homes at the north end of Holgate

Avenue and nearly into the street. Residents at the west end of First Street were evacuated from their homes by boat. The homes on the east end of First near the Public Library were also vacated. Defiance's Company G of the Ohio National Guard worked through the night sandbagging, barricading and evacuating in a storm of sleet.

Residents of the lower East Side vacated their homes as the water reached their second floors. At least 30 homes were evacuated when the water reached Second Street. Many homes on the east side of Francis St were evacuated, and all but six homes between the Hopkins Street Bridge and the Francis Street Bridge were flooded. The local moving company, Defiance Truck and Transfer was busy with their moving trucks backed up to homes on Francis Street. People began moving furniture across the street to neighbors' porches and higher ground in hopes of saving it.

Electricity was provided to the East Side by a large cable which ran across the Auglaize River on the underside of the Second Street Bridge. Electric company workers cut the lines in anticipation of the bridge possibly failing. Crews worked throughout the day burning debris piled up against the bridges to relieve the stress placed upon the structures.

Records Broken

By Tuesday, the floodwater had set a new record, breaking the one set by the flood of 1884. The Cheney Lumber Company which sat at the most northern end of the Canal, at the final lock, just before the Maumee River, was severely damaged. Workers and owners watched helplessly as vast piles of board and timber floated away in the rushing floodwaters. Just behind Cheney's sat the Harley & Whitaker Store at the northwest corner of Clinton and First featuring three floors of clothing and goods. The store was one of the largest shopping concerns in the city, and lost its entire basement full of inventory to be sold. Just north of Harley & Whitaker, Defiance Packing Company's supply of fresh produce was ruined.

The Masonic Temple, built just the year before, was flooded nearly to its basement ceiling. Businesses did what they could to help one another out. The flooded Penrod Transfer Barns moved their equipment up to the Ury Barn. The Coy and Aspacher Sawmills were completely shut down, the latter being flooded to its roof. Factories all over town were shut down because there was no controllable water to drive their machinery.

The Auglaize River Power Dam built just the year before was hobbled when bales of straw and other debris got into the grates and clogged the turbines causing it to lose power. The electricity produced there fueled many of Defiance's factories as well as the streetcars running throughout the town.

The Crescent News reported on its front page that the high waters had settled into their offices making operation of the Duplex newspaper press impossible and forcing them to reduce the paper to just four pages.

The photo, right, must have been taken after the water was receding. Court Street is in the background between the courthouse and the Italianate style commercial buildings in the background. 1913 accounts tell that the waters were so high, they had to build a plank bridge across Court Street and use a ladder to reach the Mayor's Office through a second story window.

Cropped from an Ed Bronson panoramic photo, people with an infant in front of the Defiance County Court House

Wednesday

March 26, 1913

Floods Sweep Valley! read the headline of the Defiance Crescent-News. It was a busy night as thrilling rescues were made throughout. Captain DeKay and his men in Company G of the Ohio National Guard were out most of the night with the police, firemen and other volunteers getting people out of their homes. Gas and water were lost to the entire city with no electricity on the East Side.

By 9AM the waters had risen to between twenty and twenty six feet flood stage. The water was moving over the roadway of the Second and Hopkins Street bridges. Rescue crews were working in complete darkness through the night, knocking on doors warning residents to evacuate. We've had no loss of life, but others are not so lucky. Unofficial reports were published on the front page of the Defiance Crescent-News that the Lewiston Reservoir near Dayton had failed and 30,000 are reported drowned there with 5,000 reported drowned in Dayton; thankfully this turned out to be false, but it surely added to already heightened fears. Captain DeKay and his local company of the Ohio National Guard would have been sent there, but they couldn't get a train out of Defiance. The bridges were all shut down in the night.

Water encroached on Clinton Street this Wednesday morning as far as the Court House and people rowed boats up to the square. All streets north of First were inundated with water and the lower East Side was covered with floodwaters from the 2nd Street Bridge to Seneca Street.

Robert Merrihugh, a resident of the East Side flats vacated his house yesterday and it was swept down the Auglaize River this morning. Police and fire crews rescued Frederick & Elizabeth Phelps of 103 Summit Street and the John & Henrietta Houtz family of 225 West Water Street early this morning from their homes on the East Side lowlands. Part of Alex & Ella Bruner's home in North Defiance also went down the Maumee River this morning. John Budd, a real estate agent, of 633 Frances Street (which was later renamed, Riverside Avenue), refused to leave his flooding home yesterday. Now, this morning, police, fire and militiamen (National Guard) risked their lives to rescue him.

Photo taken Wednesday morning of Second St. bridge; before the Hopkins Street Bridge washed out. National Guardsmen to the right. Postcard from Jim Hamilton Collection.

School has been canceled and the buildings have been opened to shelter those without homes. At least 75 homes in the city had been evacuated and sustained heavy damage. Conservative estimates put 100 – 150 people in need. Families reported going more than 48 hours without food and not much more than the clothes on their backs.

Mayor Schmaltz and other men met to form a Relief Association in the afternoon. Curtis M. Willock, the President of The Waverly Arms Co. and Secretary/Treasurer of The American Steel Package Company; Dr. George Edgar, and J. A. Deindoerfer of the *Defiance Herald* have been appointed to chair the committee. $1,200 was raised in fifteen minutes.

In other news, due to the flooding, the following activities were canceled: The Song Cycle at the W. C. Kegel home, and the Annual Sixth Regiment Band Concert.

Bridges
Made Fight for Bridge

The old State or "Mule" Bridge of the Miami & Erie Canal went down at 4:05 Wednesday morning. It could no longer stand the large burden of driftwood that had accumulated at its piers and the two south spans failed. That bridge was completely gone, but its piers would remain to remind boaters for the next hundred plus years of its past importance.

The Second Street Bridge held through the flood with only the railing being damaged.

The Hopkins Street Bridge had moved slightly in the night, but by 10 AM, the west span went down when it was struck by a barn coursing downriver in the floodwaters. The span floated almost to the Second Street Bridge before breaking up. By 2PM the Hopkins Bridge was entirely destroyed. See photo right.

A force of B&O men heroically "made a fight" to save the train bridge weighting it down with sandbags and keeping a loaded train on the bridge the entire time and car loads of ballast were dumped into the seething Auglaize River. A small washout occurred, but they quickly filled it in.

Francis Street, shown at left looking north, was hard hit. The flood tore out the street leaving the sewer exposed, eight feet below. The approach to the Francis Street Bridge which then crossed the Auglaize River was completely washed away. The Francis Street Bridge was lost, never to be rebuilt.

Postcards offered from Jim Hamilton and Jo McCormick Collections

PKL...ST BRIDGE SPAN LEAVING

Below: This photo was shot after the first section of the Hopkins Street Bridge washed out. The remaining span is seen to the left on this page. In the background, the B&O Train is parked on the railroad bridge to add weight giving the bridge more strength in the raging flood waters and the large amounts of debris being carried downstream. Photographer unknown.

Left: Notice the men walking precariously along the tracks and over the waters. Jo McCormick Collection.

Hopkins St Bridge 41

Captain DeKay

Albert DeKay had been in the service of the National Guard prior to 1904 when he fought in the Spanish American War. He made his home in Defiance in 1902 when, in time, an idea began to circulate to form a National Guard Unit. Albert DeKay jumped at the idea. General McMaken of the Ohio National Guard visited Defiance and was presented with the idea and promptly proclaimed it couldn't be done. Later, Colonel Howard, commander of the Sixth Regiment was persuaded to visit. He agreed wholeheartedly with General McMaken, a unit could not be formed in Defiance. Our Albert DeKay could not be dissuaded and got permission to circulate information and try to recruit. DeKay's passionate belief and firm persistence convinced the Colonel to grant the request. DeKay worked tirelessly to recruit the required enlistment and soon Defiance was represented as Company G of the Sixth Ohio Regiment under its leader, Captain Albert DeKay. Crescent-News February 12, 1910.

DeKay went on to serve in the Ohio National Guard for 33 years becoming the oldest Ohio captain to lead a company of fighting men overseas when he left for France in WWI. He led Defiance men through labor strikes, flood response, patrolling the Mexico border and fought in the trenches in WWI. Albert DeKay was also an avid baseball enthusiast and umpired for the local league. When Company G was renamed Company "A" and reclassified as a howitzer unit complete with mules in 1921, Captain DeKay knew it was time to retire.

Captain Albert B. DeKay
Ohio National Guard
Company G. Founder

"Militia Boys Do Good Work"

Ohio National Guard

At the turn of the last century, the terms militia and National Guard are used almost interchangeably. This can cause some confusion if we don't understand the history of our military. When Ohio gained its statehood, it was required to form a militia as had all the other previously existing states. Most states required men between the ages of eighteen and forty five to be a part of the State Militia which was meant to defend the state from attack. The first half of the 19th century saw little in the way of threats to Ohio as the native people had been "removed" and peaceful relations were well established with England, France and Canada. Ohio greatly reduced its funding to a state militia.

In 1846, the US went to war with Mexico. Then the Civil War broke out in April of 1861. Governor Dennison sent George McClellan and Jacob Cox to the state arsenal where they found non-functioning cannons, and some old muskets. With little of value to the state, the Governor urged communities to revive their militia system and form units. These

groups went to Columbus where they were quickly trained to act as a professional fighting force of volunteers.

After the Civil War, the Ohio Militia once again saw a decline. Private armies were assembled and paid by early industrialists to protect their factories and investments. By the 1890's "private armies" such as the Pinkertons outnumbered the standing Army of the entire United States. Ohio saw this as such a threat that they outlawed the Pinkertons altogether.

In 1903, the United States formally created the National Guard, mostly because the condition of the State Militias was so poor. States would still oversee their National Guard units and the units were trained primarily to work within their state at times of state emergency, but now the Federal Government had the authority to activate National Guard units and send them where needed, even to other countries.

Defiance's own Company G. was formed in the fall of 1904.

Thursday

March 27, 1913

The flood waters reached their crest at 3AM Thursday morning topping out at 26 feet. They held their record swell and then began to fall at 4 in the afternoon.

Seventy Five to 100 families were homeless just on the east side plus 50 more in other parts of town. About 15 east-siders with nowhere else to go, moved into the school there. The schools, the Presbyterian Church on Washington Avenue, St. Paul's Methodist at Third and Wayne, and the Baptist Church at 323 Wayne were all opened to the homeless.

Flood relief was at the top of Defiance's priorities. The Crescent-News reported talking to a man who had nothing left but the suit on his back. His family had nothing to eat for 48 hours. He was not alone in his plight. It will take at least a week to clean up the devastation of the flood, the paper goes on to report.

The corner Sample Room of the Crosby Hotel at Third & Wayne was set up as Flood Relief Headquarters. Cots, bedding and cash were most urgently needed. A fleet of wagons were made ready to go and pick up donations. "This is a time when all must get together as one big family and assist those who have been temporarily made homeless by the muddy waters," urged The Crescent-News

The Presbyterian Church on Washington Avenue where the Holgate and Turnbull families attended and the St. Paul's Methodist Church attended by the Kettenring Family and Charles Slocum both had kitchens and steam boiling plants made ready for the homeless to stay and eat until their homes were repaired. Cots were set up there.

"If you know of anyone in need, report them to the Headquarters at the Crosby. If you wish to show the proper spirit to our fellowmen and can afford it, donate either money or cots and bed-clothing. Both are badly needed." Crescent News

Good News! The waters were receding; bad news! It snowed. The receding of the muddy, yellow waters was followed by several inches of pure, white snow adding to the suffering of those made homeless by the high waters. Mayor Schmaltz issued a warning to all citizens to guard against fire. There was still no water pressure in the city and a fire would greatly add to the present disaster. There was also no gas in the city and no electric to the East Side.

The Village of Florida, just outside Defiance County, was reported completely under water and the residents all living in the school house up on the hill. They lost several buildings in the flood waters.

Ed Bronson photo of the Crosby Hotel, downtown Defiance on the north side of Third Street. The Crosby had always been a hub of activity for special occasions. It became the center for flood relief and business reorganization.

Pianos & Movers

The piano was the number one source of home entertainment in homes of society and class at the time of the flood. Far more girls were taught to play piano than boys, yet women were discouraged from pursuing piano as a career. A girl's ability to play the piano was directly correlated to her suitability for marriage. Pianos became a status symbol for the fast emerging American middle class.

The 1910 Defiance City Directory shows two piano dealers in town: Fullers Music Store and Hale Piano at 408 and 313 Clinton Street respectively.

When the flood waters came, there was a fury of moving and trying to save furniture with the piano being one of the greatest investments. Many families were renting their piano or purchasing it on

Right: Fuller's Music Store at 408 Clinton Street was one of two piano dealers listed in the 1910 Defiance Directory. Hale Piano at 313 Clinton was the other.

Left: Ad placed in Smith's Defiance Directory 1910 inside cover.

DEFIANCE TRUCK & TRANSFER CO.

R. C. PACKER, Proprietor

DRAYING and MOVING

QUICK DELIVERY ❧ BEST SERVICE
RIGHT CHARGES

FULLER'S MUSIC STORE,
DEFIANCE, O.
ESTABLISHED 1885.

finance terms from the local dealers. Pianos were monstrous uprights weighing in the neighborhood of 500 to 700 pounds.

Later, the next week, the Defiance Crescent-News front page contained a Notice To The Public: "In denial of the report that the Defiance Truck & Transfer has been charging $6 to move a piano from the flooded district, Mr. Packer states that when it was necessary to use four men to move a piano out of water, $2.50 was charged and when two men could do the work only $2 was charged. Anyone who had paid more than this is asked to call at the office of the company."

"A Piano Hospital for Flood Pianos" was the headline in The Crescent News, April 3, 1913. The paper reported that Fuller's Music Store employees and "truck men" of the Defiance Truck & Transfer Company hustled last week to remove many pianos from homes as the water was so rapidly rising. They want dearly to try and save as many pianos as possible and so have started a piano hospital in a room of D. Lieber's hay and clover seed store.

Firemen

We hear grand reports about our Firemen who were on the job! They worked from early morning to late at night helping rescue people from their flooded homes. Firemen were carrying furniture, and loading and unloading moving vans well into the night. Many other citizens joined in volunteering their time and strength in the cause. They all "manifest the proper spirit and are due the thanks of many." Crescent News Thursday

Defiance City Council set up the first fire department on September 1, 1872 and it was all volunteer. Early equipment was manpower and one steam pumper able to build a full head of 90 pound steam in just 15 minutes and throw water over 200 feet. John F. Deatrick was the first volunteer fire chief, which they then called Chief Engineer. Louis Spring was the longest serving volunteer Chief Engineer with 30 years from 1888 to 1918 when John Scheuerman became the first paid Fire Chief, working for 13 years in that position.

It was Spring who built the blueprint for the fire alarm system. Twenty Gamewell fire alarm boxes were placed throughout the city. Gamewells were in just 250 cities in 1886 and doubled to 500 by 1890. Scheuerman's tenure saw the gasoline motor enter the firefighting scene. Defiance's earliest "truck" was a Buick passenger car overhauled by the Defiance Carriage Company for fire service. Soon the Defiance Motor Truck Company got in on the action, eventually changing their name to the Century Motor Truck Company. One of their models was converted and outfitted for fire service. That truck still exists in Defiance at this printing.

Cor 3rd & Jackson 13

Right and Left, postcards from the Jim Hamilton and Jo McCormick collections.

Friday

March 28, 1913

As if the flooding wasn't bad enough, one of the highest winds yet to sweep our corner of the world descended upon the area early this morning. "High winds wrecked bill boards, telegraph and telephone wires and poles. Defiance Hall's roof over at the college is missing a good portion, as is St. Paul's Methodist, the Y.V.E.T.O.T. Club and National Union Hall. The Defiance Street Railway lost a long line of trolley wire which will be a heavy loss. The Turnbull lost power to the blacksmith shop. The large silo at the Latchaw Dairy Farm blew over with Lon Phillips in it! Tinners, line men, hardware men and repair men are in demand as never before!" (Crescent News). The newspaper continued to report:

Ohio Governor Cox declared a ten day holiday for all the flood stricken areas giving forgiveness which applied to notes, mortgages and the like becoming due during that time.

The number of homeless in Defiance has risen to 200 - money is needed. The local relief funds reached $2,500 with more arriving every hour. C. M. Willock of the Relief Committee was forced to leave work Thursday as he suffered a breakdown from the mental strain of overwork throughout this crisis. More members have been appointed. Cots, bedding, clothing and money are in dire need.

The Gas company reports that they are underway in clearing the water from the gas main. They should be able to restore service Saturday or Sunday. They are hoping to have electric lights restored to the East Side Saturday. The Electric Company has a large force of men at work. They kept the lights on in central Defiance throughout the flood.

Governor Cox phoned Mayor Schmaltz directing Company G to work under the mayor's orders until the mayor decided they were no longer needed. A number of Ohio National Guardsmen patrolled the flood district Thursday night to prevent looting that was reported in Thursday's paper. They have orders to shoot any suspicious characters. Their guns are loaded.

The rivers have receded enough to allow pedestrians to be ferried across Front Street (now Fort Street) to the Clinton Street Bridge where they can cross the Maumee on foot. Company G is of great help and has worked tirelessly through the rain and sleet and all through the night. Sergeant Alltoffer has even managed to deliver the mail to Defiance College this morning!

Rumors the Turnbull will close are false. The plant will be employing men again to start the cleanup next week.

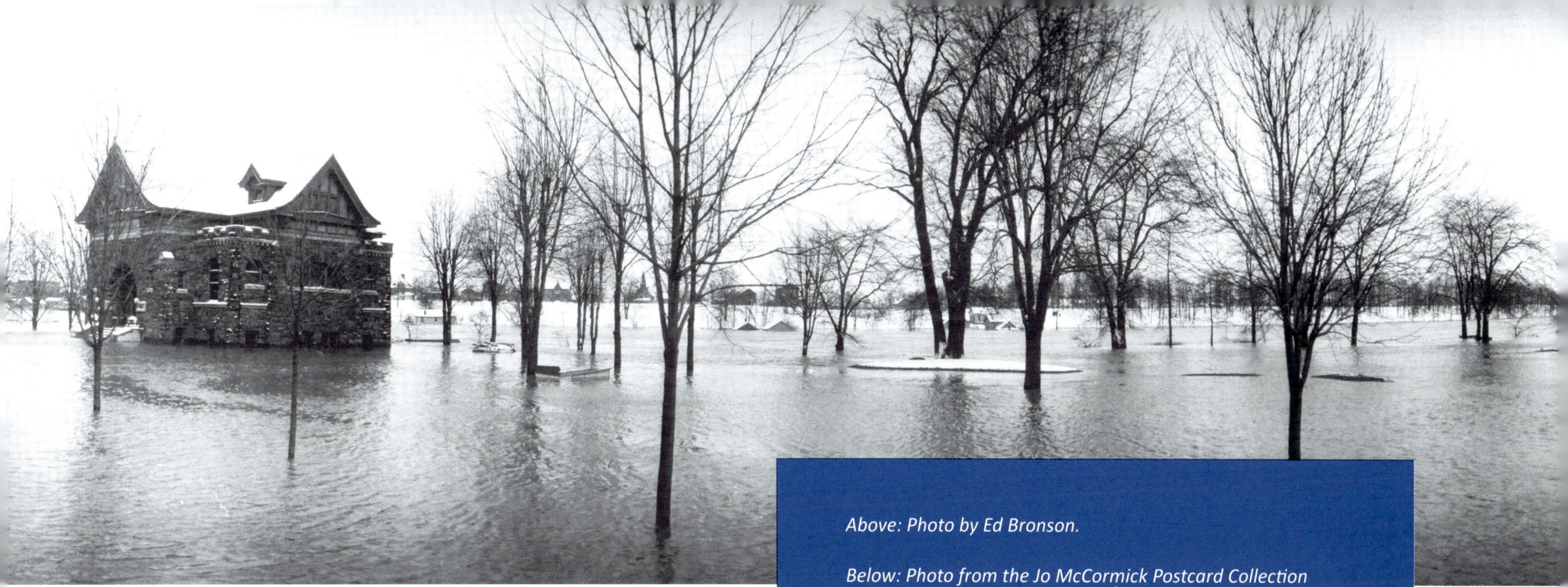

Above: Photo by Ed Bronson.

Below: Photo from the Jo McCormick Postcard Collection

The Defiance Public Library Recorded the following in their Board Minutes:

"This brings the week of the great flood. The regular meeting was dispensed with at noon on Tuesday March 25th. The water had flooded the fire-room putting out the furnace fire and thereby necessitating the closing of the library. By Wednesday morning all approaches to the building were impassable except by boat. By Thursday morning the entire fort grounds were under water and the water in the basement had risen to a height of seven feet. At its crest, the water had covered all but three of the stone steps at the front entrance to the building. By order of the Board of Health the library will be kept closed for two weeks."

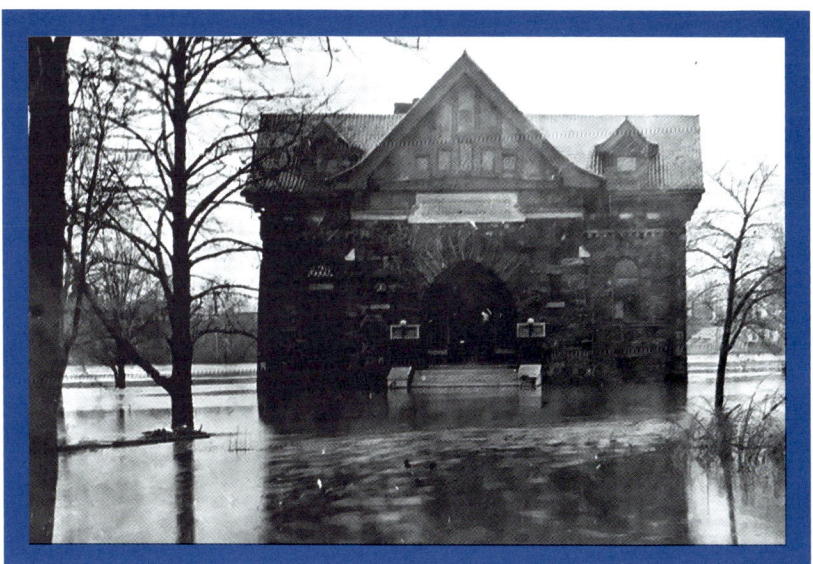

It was several days before the Crescent News could use its presses that were completely covered in water during the flood. The Defiance Printing & Engraving Co. was kind enough to print the paper from their shop while the Crescent set its type by hand. Since the gas was cut off, the Linotype machines were out of business. Sadly, Fred Stever, cashier of Merchants National Bank, was seriously ill with typhoid fever. His house is the one below directly behind the canoe. His home was flooded at the same time that he fell ill. He was taken four doors down to the home of W. C. Holgate, grandson to William C. Holgate, who had ridden on horseback to Columbus petitioning for the creation of Defiance County, to recover. How generous of Mr. Holgate - a true friend. W. C. Holgate's brother, Robert was the Vice President of the same bank.

Typhoid fever was a big concern during and after the flood. The typhoid that Fred Stever was experiencing probably was not from flood water. Typhoid is caused by Salmonella typhi bacteria and takes one to three weeks to develop. Defiance had city sewers which were flooded and even exposed spilling more than usual levels of raw sewage into the rivers and flood waters. In 1910, typhoid fever was the 7th highest cause of death in the United States following consumption, pneumonia (tuberculosis), heart disease, diarrheal disease, unknown causes and disease of the kidney.

Left: Ed Bronson Collection.

Right: postcard, Jo McCormick Collection

EAST FROM ST MARYS

Utilities

Municipal utilities, still in their infancy in 1913, were heavily impacted by the floods. The Auglaize Power Company was hit hard when water cut through at the ends of their new power house south of town on the Auglaize River. Friday morning about 10:45, the embankment to the west of the Power Dam gave way. Water rushed through the Schneider farm. Defiance rang the courthouse bell and the fire bell that morning when it was reported that the entire Power Dam had gone out. They rang the bells in warning, but it was only the west bank that completely collapsed.

The Crescent reported: "The Defiance Water company pumping stations were flooded yesterday. Defiance lost water pressure throughout the city. Water was turned back on Saturday night, March 29th after the workmen cleared the pump station of debris. Gas was also back on Saturday. East side still without electric light. The main part of town never lost electric light, but the cables across to the East side were cut when the water reached the bridges they ran across on," (Sunday paper).

Below, note the large chunk of concrete to the left and then the large gap and more concrete on the right. That is the hole the floodwaters tore through the retaining wall of the dam. Note the man standing on the boulder in the center of the 120 foot gap in below photo. Photo from Ed Bronson Collection.

Ed Bronson photo details the severe contours worn into the farm field from the flood waters.

Auglaize Power Company

Defiance first got electric light in 1881 when it was installed at the Turnbull Wagon Works. A year later, the Turnbull became a stock company with Toledo based investors employing four to five hundred men. It was one of the largest employers in Defiance and run by very forward thinking and industrious people who grew a simple agricultural wheel manufacturer into wagon making, then buggies and carriages and eventually automobiles. They built their entire business using machines and tools made at the Defiance Machine Works.

Incandescent light of 500-16 candlepower lamps, free of smoke and soot was now available in Defiance from the Defiance Electric Light Company. In the early 1900's they began plans for a power dam on the Auglaize River above Defiance, but did not realize the dream until 1911 when the Auglaize Power Company was incorporated. The dam was completed in May 1912, and the power house done a few weeks later employing 103 men at the peak of construction. Near completion, an intense dispute arose over who should distribute the current and at what price. Over budget, the investors fought for higher rates than Defiance had envisioned. Negotiations between Auglaize Power Company and Defiance Gas & Electric ended, and a group of Defiance businessmen incorporated Defiance Utilities Company which city council granted a franchise, but rates were still way too high.

Then came the Great 1913 Flood, tearing a gap 120 feet wide through the west wing embankment, leaving 65 - 75 acres of the John Schneider farm's bottom land swept completely clean of soil down to the rock, measuring 15 feet deep in places. After all that damage, many investors just wanted to sell. In January of 1914, John Schneider and John W. Schneider brought suit against the Auglaize Power Dam Company claiming faulty construction caused the tear and that his 250 acre farm valued at $150 an acre was devalued to just $75 an acre. The suit went on for two years. No resolution was ever reported in the newspapers.

The primary investor in the Auglaize Power Company bought out the Defiance Gas & Electric Company the Auglaize Power Company, the Maumee Valley Light and Power and the local utility creating a company that was subsequently bought out by Toledo Edison in 1924. The Auglaize Dam hydro electric plant generated 5,000 kilowatts with round the clock operations until 1962.

In the photo to the right, a man assumed to be John Schneider points across his devastated farmland toward the Auglaize Power Dam which stands on the other side of the river from him. His farm and barns in the background are directly opposite the Power Dam and the silo still stand there today.

Saturday

March 29, 1913

The City of Toledo telephoned to announce they were donating $2,000 cash and 100 cots and blankets. The local relief fund had reached $2,500 and there were high hopes to raise another $1,000. "Here is the time to show the real spirit that makes a town, in time of disaster." That would bring the total to $5,000 which is the bare minimum needed.

The board of health has ordered that no flooded homes can be entered without permission. Notices were posted on all flooded homes to this effect in hopes of stopping disease.

Captain DeKay of Company G requested citizens to identify themselves to the guardsman when out at night or in their own yards as Company G was under orders to patrol and fire on looters. "Citizens must boil their water when it is restored to them within the flood district, scrub the floors with liquid soap and apply lime to their basement floors," (Crescent News Saturday).

It was thought that the rivers would probably return to normal by

Below: Looking out toward the B&O Bridge and Auglaize River from St. Mary's Church steeple. Photo by Ed Bronson.

Saturday night according to the newspaper. The paper also reported that the fall was slower last night than anticipated. In actuality, the rivers would not return to their banks until Monday which shows the extent of flooding throughout the entire Maumee watershed.

On a brighter note, the Cheney Lumber Company didn't fair as badly as feared. The heroic men employed there built a large boom which was a masterpiece of ingenuity. It saved their stock of timber and buildings from being washed away. The Saturday paper reported hopes to "have the gas back on tonight and water tonight or Sunday." Street cars resumed this morning. Public school will resume Monday. The picture theaters of the city will give a benefit show Sunday afternoon and night. Admission is a free-will offering. The forty hours devotion scheduled at St. Mary's Church was postponed. The Poultry Association Hall also opened to the homeless.

Below, man in black trench coat is identified as Don Switzer, a bookkeeper at Defiance Machine Works. He lived nearby at 317 Jefferson. The taller man in lighter hat (third from left) is Lloyd Tuttle the popular Crescent News "Backward Glance" writer. Photo by Ed Bronson.

Flood Relief

Dr. Robert Cameron, Merl Goller & Emery Lattanner were in charge of post flood relief in Defiance and worked from the Crosby House Hotel. Donations were stored and distributed from St. Paul Methodist Church's first floor. They appealed to Governor Cox and received cots, mattresses, blankets and dishes via train from Chicago. Cash was issued by the government to the Red Cross for relief aid. The Red Cross did not yet have a presence in Defiance in 1913. They "seek to help the ones that need it the most, which in all cases are the laboring people who do not own homes and whose household furniture has been ruined or carried away," (Emery Lattanner, April 1st letter in Defiance Crescent April 2, 1913). These men were traveling to Columbus via automobile to seek relief for Defiance citizens which was at least a 16 hour trip each way in 1913. As of this printing, one can drive, from Defiance to the Maine coast in that time.

Mayor Schmaltz received a telephone call from Sherwood Friday morning offering to send men over and assist with the cleanup, or anything else they could do to help. The tiny village of neighboring Jewell also started raising a relief fund. Schmaltz received a telegram from Toledo's Mayor offering free hospital service in Toledo, $2,000 in cash and 100 cots and blankets. Toledo was not greatly affected by the flood. The Lion Theater advertised Sunday's moving picture proceeds would benefit the Relief Fund. Wells Fargo carried money and supplies into Defiance at no charge to support the relief effort.

Money was raised and sent to Defiance from Hicksville, Sherwood, Jewell, Bryan, VanWert, and Toledo. Disinfectant Soap was sent in, with supplies quickly exhausted. The newspapers assured more was on its way at no charge. The Health Board advised "Boil all water, sprinkle the mud with lime and scrub the house well with liquid soap" (Defiance Crescent-News April 1, 1913). The Munsingwear Store advertised a 10% discount to flood sufferers and assured their goods were dry and undamaged by the flood. It was speculated in the newspaper that "portioned to the wealth and population of the cities struck by the flood Defiance was hit harder than Dayton" (Crescent News).

All three theaters in Defiance allowed the Y.V.E.T.O.T. Club to organize a flood relief effort and showed movies Sunday March 30 with all proceeds going to flood relief. Tuesday, April 1st, the theater troupe of "The Spring Maid" donated 25 percent of their gross receipts at the Defiance Opera House and the Defiance Club raffled an automobile that night at the theater.

Postcard from Jim Hamilton Collection.

Cleanup Begins

Our Golden Era of Industry

The Defiance County Board of Health issued the following order: "All water from wells and cisterns in the district must be boiled. The water contains typhoid fever germs and all citizens must boil their water before drinking or there will be a typhoid breakout."

The paper advised that floors should be well scrubbed with "Green Soap", a liquid soap. They perhaps referred to Palmolive which was in production at the time of the flood and had a green color that came from the palm, olive and cocoa butter oils it was made of. It further stated, cellars should be thoroughly scrubbed down and lime sprinkled about. Lime was the cheapest and best disinfectant that could be secured. People in the flood district must boil all water, even for washing. This instruction "should be obeyed to the letter."

Ad from the Crescent News at the end of the flood.
Mr. Willock had been in charge of the initial flood response.

Photo by Ed Bronson, is zoomed in to see the northwest corner of Second and Seneca. Most of these buildings still stand as of this publication.

Tuesday

April 1, 1913

The Crescent-News, Tuesday reported the following:

Representatives from Toledo's Police & Fire Departments and its Commerce Club visited Defiance to see how Toledo could help. They are visiting all area flood stricken cities and will donate to Fremont, Tiffin, Findlay and others. They've already sent clothing, supplies, plus 150 cots and blankets. Defiance is requesting $5,000 in cash. Hicksville sent $350 which is greatly appreciated. 268 homes here are flooded and judged uninhabitable by the Health Department. Conservative estimates put the loss here to at least five to six million dollars.

National Guardsmen are still on patrol and "taking in tramps." Anyone out after 10PM will be challenged by the guardsmen as to their intentions. Three Whites and three Negroes who could not give account for themselves were taken into the county jail over the weekend where they will stay until it is safe to get out of town.

Winterich Greenhouse, (now Kirchers) thanks those who helped him heat the greenhouses for two days with temporary oil burners due to the boiler flooding there.

A. Goldnetz refutes the story, that he has raised meat prices. Rather, he has given freely to those worthy or applied liberal discounts to those in need. His books are open to the Relief Committee for inspection.

Northwestern and Bell telephone companies are working to repair damaged lines. Telephones that were under water are being dried in the Tenzer Lumber Company dry kilns and will be reinstalled as soon as possible.

The Board of Health has placed 50 sacks of lime at Fred Wolsiffer's place at 208 East Second St. There is more available at Defiance Packing Company, Defiance Creamery and Frank Humberts at 640 Washington. Disinfectant soap can be gotten at the Central Fire Station; free to all who need it.

By April 4th, nearly 1,000 people were displaced from their homes. 300 families had lost all their household goods and many of them, their homes.

"Telephone Girls"
Thanks Extended

The telephone was a fairly new invention in 1913, but it proved itself invaluable and ensured its place in the world during crises such as the flood. Stories about of the heroic men and women who kept their posts for days on end throughout the ordeal flooded the country. The position was largely held by women who were called "Telephone Girls" or "Hello Girls" despite the fact that most were mature, married women and mothers.

The Crescent-News proclaimed that all were grateful to the "Telephone Girls" who handled a multitude of calls through the crisis and worked overtime to make sure calls went through. The local telephone operators are to be commended. "This paper and its correspondents to the city dailies feel very grateful to the girls for their faithfulness in discharging their duties by day and night."

The 1910 Defiance City Directory lists the following: Central Union Telephone Company at 609-11 Third Street, Northwestern Telephone Company 522 1/2 Clinton Street, Postal Telegraph-Cable Company at 523 Second Street and Western Union Telegraph Company located at 317 Third Street.

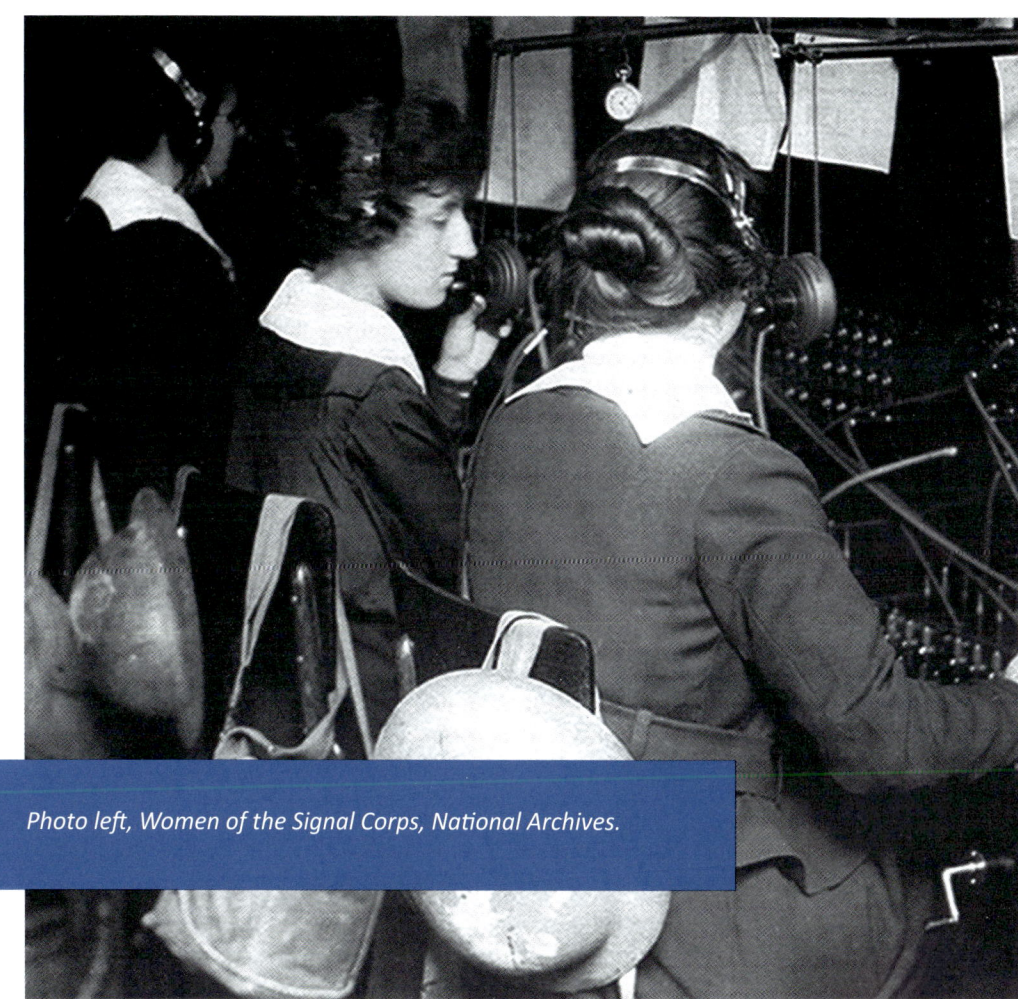

Photo left, Women of the Signal Corps, National Archives.

Keeping Business Afloat

Defiance Weathers the Storm

Lumber still was a big industry in Defiance, even in the early 1900's. The lumber from Cheney Lumber, on the riverbank near the mule bridge has washed to First and Wayne According to the Wednesday, April 2nd Crescent News, they'd lost thousands of dollars in materials. "The Turnbull Wagon Works will lose between $40,000 and $50,000 in lumber."

The Turnbull Wagon Works, Defiance's largest employer, had water over the floor of their main shop. The Turnbull occupied about six blocks of the city's east side on the Maumee River east of Kingsbury Park and extended nearly to the stream known as Preston Run. On Friday the Turnbull factory had set up an office in the Crosby House Hotel and announced that it was absolutely not going under due to the flood and that work would resume the next week. That next Tuesday, 21 men, mostly farmers, showed up at the Turnbull yards and worked the entire day gratis, assisting with cleanup of debris. These men knew the Turnbull was hard hit and appreciate what the factory

Wreck of the Diehl Brick Yards Drying Racks - Ed Bronson

meant to the town. Many of them worked there during the winter months to supplement their harvest income.

The basement of the Harley & Whitaker Store, at the now vacant corner of First and Clinton Street was completely flooded. Across the street, Hoffman Furniture Store also lost much inventory. Defiance Creamery, along the river, lost the back wall of the creamery.

J.F. Singer Grocery Company, Kehnast & Smith and all the stores north of the Court House Square had great loss. The Compo Garage, Diehl Brewing Company, Garvey & Company, and Diehl Brick and Tile all cleaned up a great mess. Water on Perry Street reached within half a block of Defiance Machine Works and City Hall. The Ury Barn was vacated and all the horses removed. Of note: "Charles Latchaw will still be delivering milk to his customers. Those with infants can secure milk at Wrede's Meat Market Wednesday."

Crescent News Ad

The Ice House

The flood wiped out Millers Ice Houses, Shoemaker-Greaser Company, and most other ice houses along the rivers and took with it the winter harvest of ice packed away in sawdust in rambling wooden structures dotting the banks of the river and canal, standing ready for use by nearby industry. A good ice supplier would harvest about 6,000 tons of ice and hold that supply for use throughout the summer and stretching it until the next winter season. The January papers of 1913 had reported serious deficiencies in ice collection as it had been a warmer winter with above average rainfalls and swollen rivers. Even if they'd managed to fill the ice houses in February, the March flood caused Defiance to find itself, suddenly, without ice and with little hope for recovery. By Monday of the week following the flood, the Defiance Democrat and Defiance Crescent-News were both featuring front page articles concerning the organization of the Defiance Ice Company to manufacture artificial ice with a capacity of 10 tons. Stock subscriptions were already coming in so rapidly, the organizers decided to increase the capacity of the plant to 15-20 tons of ice a day. They expected to be making ice in about 30 days. The venture was a success and one more modern innovation spurred from the 1913 disaster.

Trolley

In 1887, Defiance built an electric street railway connecting the B&O railroad depot at Harrison and Deatrick Streets to the downtown. A wooden car barn was at the southeast corner of Harrison and Fifth. A small depot building still stands near there today. The original line ran up Harrison to Third, turning east and passing under the Wabash train viaduct. It continued over a swing bridge then crossed the open Miami & Erie Canal, then turned north onto Clinton Street and ran on to First Street where it turned around. An extension was built at Third and Clinton that took the trolley south on Clinton to Juliet Street where it headed east to Jefferson, took a short jog north, and then east again on Fifth Street which turns into Hopkins Street at the bridge. Crossing the Hopkins Street bridge, the trolley then terminated at Ottawa Avenue at the East Side Fire Station, Gushman Restaurant (which later became Maag's) and then the clubhouse for the East Defiance Citizens Band.

A third addition continued the street car line further east on Hopkins over a rickety and precipitous trestle crossing Preston Run Ravine to Squires Avenue. South on Squire a short way ended the trolley service at the B&O railroad again.

The final expansion continued west on Hopkins, turned north on Richland Street, crossed Second Street and ended at the river where passengers could exit the Trolley and take the floating pontoon foot bridge across to the Island Park.

The trolley seen above and below left as it crosses Preston Run on Defiance's east side.

Photo below is at west Third and Clinton Streets.
Ed Bronson Collection.

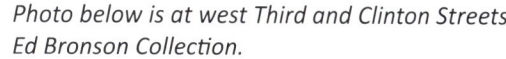

Island Park

Today's Preston Island, then called "Island Park" is still a magical place. Occasionally the meandering waters of the river part, yielding an outcropping of high ground isolated from the hustle and bustle of the world, suspended in time, free of human habitation. One such outcropping stands just over a mile east of our beautiful confluence. It was once explored by the prehistoric, ancient tribes, now lost to myth, who took their turns nomadically traveling and hunting up and down the bountiful banks of the great river we call the Maumee. The Island, as it came to be known, was thirty some acres in size, a large hill rising up from the placid waters as if for some special or hallowed purpose.

As the days of rough-hewn canoes and pirogues came to an end, the river instead became highway to the excursion boat, the pleasure yacht and the steamer. The Island was discovered again as a paradise for rest, culture and recreation; a beacon to all who were "weary and heavy laden". July 28, 1900 saw the then 30 acres yield to the orchestrated joys of a summer Chautauqua series held in a 700 seat auditorium; baseball and football fields, a half mile race track for cars, bicycles and horses, lawn tennis, croquet, a restaurant, refreshment stands, a pavilion for dancing, a merry-go-round, a shooting gallery, penny arcade and more. An island of pleasure was in reach, just a short trolley car or steamer boat ride from Defiance, the most industrious city in the Maumee Valley.

Entertainment on the island was diverse. The summer Chautauqua of 1903, for example, saw a series of lecturers, magicians, quartets of singers, bell ringers, "bird imitation and warbling" and, separate from the Chautauqua performances, an automobile race. One of the largest draws of the summer came with an address by U.S. Senator and Presidential candidate William Jennings Bryan.

Three wells were drilled on the island furnishing drinking water. Refreshments included peanuts, lemonade, candy and ice cream. Packed picnic baskets were enjoyed in the picnic grove. The original Rube Band and local semi-professional baseball teams all made regular appearance on the Island. A hotel and plenty of tent camping made for convenient summer accommodations.

The Flood of 1913 washed away most of the Island structures. One account in Napoleon claimed they watched the carousel horses float past and under the bridge in Napoleon during the height of the flood. Currently the island measures closer to 23 acres. Surely the difference can be explained by heavy losses of ground in the rushing floodwaters of 1913 and subsequent severe floods.

Island Park

Defiance

Hopkins Street Bridge

Two days after losing the Hopkins Street Bridge, citizens were already thinking of how to pay for the replacement. Friday's Crescent News wrote on the front page that the Ohio Electric Railway may help the county to rebuild the bridge and a representative would be in Defiance soon.

The Defiance County Commissioners awarded the bridge contract to W. I. Rath who hired all local workers. The bridge cost $56,000 and was the most expensive improvement ever done in the county. They also laid street car rails in the bridge to the south side in anticipation of the street car running again. The rails were paid for by the Defiance Holding Company whose manager was also secretary of the newly formed Chamber of Commerce as a gesture of optimism for Defiance.

The bridge was finished in the fall of 1914 and would last until 1983. Many stories survive from east side residents who walked, as youngsters, the wood slatted bridge to school with many sidewalk slats precariously missing.

THE New Hopkins Street Bridge W-I-Rath Contractor C.H.Bock Erector Bronson 1914

All three Hopkins St Bridge Photos from the Ed Bronson Collection.

THE NEW HOPKINS STREET BRIDGE

FIRST DAY OVER THE NEW HOPKINS STREET BRIDGE SATURDAY OCT-31- 1914

The End of the Canals

The canals were a short lived innovation that made Ohio the industrial epicenter of America's industrial revolution. Charted in 1837, and hand dug by hundreds, if not thousands of mostly immigrant laborers, the canal opened Defiance to trade by 1845. There were six locks in or near Defiance. Those locks slowed down traffic and caused Defiance to prosper. For ten booming years the canal drove Defiance's economy until it was gradually replaced by the faster and more dependable year-round railroads by 1855. Passenger traffic moved to the railroad almost immediately. In 1908, the state legislature authorized an expenditure of $500,000 to dig the canals deeper and rehab them. In Defiance, they rebuilt the locks with concrete and reinforced the "mule bridge" over the Maumee. The canal still lagged compared to the days when directionally opposing Captains physically fought one another to win the right to enter the canal first. The 1913 Flood ended all of that.

The 1913 Flood tore up or destroyed enough of the canal that it was all but abandoned. There was still talk of re-digging a "high speed" canal line from Cincinnati and the Ohio River all the way up to Toledo's port on Lake Erie, but that project never came to fruition. The canal sat abandoned, collecting trash and debris and serving as nothing more than a general nuisance until it was filled in about 1917 within the city of Defiance.

"Municipalities have the burden of caring for the unfortunate and the more extensive problem of rebuilding with a greatly decreased tax duplicate.

"Bonds will have to be sold to raise the funds. There is no other way of financing. Bonds are slow sale in Ohio. Public ownership of utilities, home rule and franchise revocation all open problems to bond buyers. Investors take no chances. The problem of refinancing may thus become doubly serious.

"There is talk that an amendment to the state constitution, exempting from taxation municipal bonds, will be submitted to the legislature next week. Members of that body claim such a provision is mandatory and that financing cannot reasonably be done without it." (Defiance Democrat April 1, 1913, p. 4)

Photo right taken June 4th 1902 of a small but complete raft of around 11,760 cubic feet of shiptimber, (squared oak timber). Charles Slocum claimed this was the last of the great shiptimber industry to pass through Defiance. The complete raft included a shanty where the cooking and lodging took place, carrying hay on its roof for the horses drawing the raft through the Maumee River and the Miami & Erie Canal. This photo is shot from the Clinton Street Bridge looking southeast toward the fort grounds. Photo from Charles Slocum's book "History of the Maumee River Basin"

100 Years Later

Historic Homes of Defiance researchers Trish Sanford-Speiser and Cam Williams were working on a National Register Nomination for the neighborhood in Defiance's First Plat near the library and fort grounds when they kept running into old Crescent News articles and other information mentioning the 1913 Flood. "Rich Rozevink told us that he had a file of newspaper articles he had collected from the Flood. He made us copies of what he had and we were hooked on the story," Trish states.

The Rover Pipeline Grant became available in Defiance about the same time as the idea to mark the flood height and tell the story of that great flood. The grant and many generous donations of time, talent and labor made the project a reality. According to 1913 Crescent News information, the people of that time planned to place "tablets" at the library and the Court House showing how high the water had risen and felt it was important to remember what the rivers could do and how they could absolutely paralyze a community. As far as we know, that was not done until now. The team of volunteers from Historic Homes worked for a year and a half to have recycled city street light poles refurbished into flood poles and installed at the confluence of the Maumee and Auglaize Rivers. One stands just past

left field at Kingsbury Park; one is on the riverbank at the fort-grounds overlooking the Auglaize and one is near the boat launch at Pontiac Park. Interpretive signage was placed at each pole telling the story of the flood. A fourth interpretive sign was placed at the corner of First and Wayne near the Post Office with a photo taken of the flooded neighborhood from that exact same spot in 1913. Historic Homes will also dedicate a page to the 1913 Flood on their new website at www.HistoricHomesofDefiance.com telling the complete story.

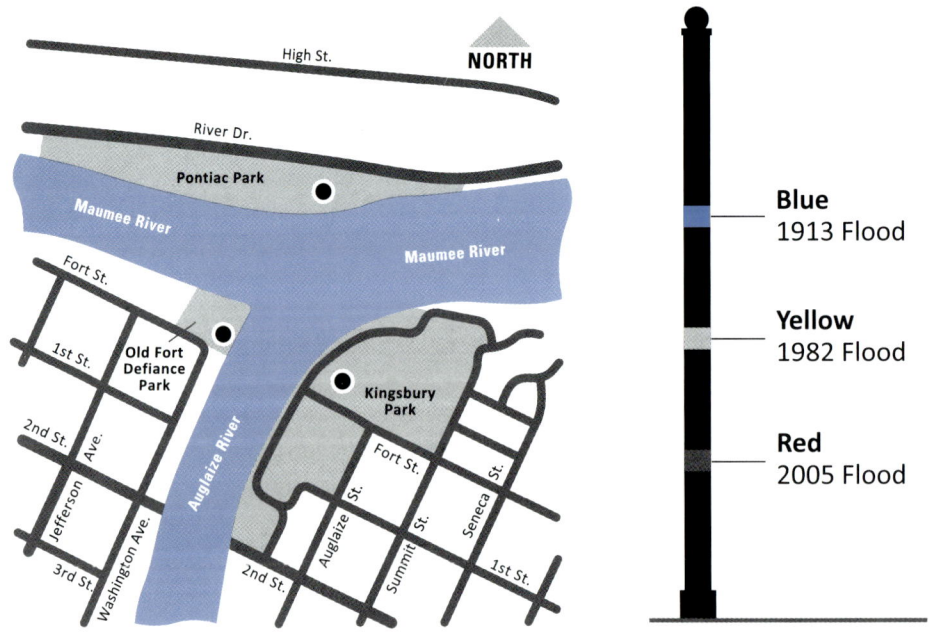

The End of the Flood

The Flood of 1913 forever changed Defiance and the other cities experiencing its force. It ended the canal system in Ohio, changed the way public works projects were funded and forced frontier towns like Defiance, to modernize their infrastructure. Politically, The Vonderheide Act, also known as the Ohio Conservancy Law was passed in 1914. It was challenged in the Ohio State Supreme Court in 1915 and the U.S. Supreme Court in 1919, (see Orr V. Allen), but upheld each time. The law gave authority to the State of Ohio to establish watershed districts and to then raise funds for improvements of those districts. The Miami Conservancy District down in Dayton, Ohio was created in 1915 thanks to the law and became the first substantial district of its kind in the nation. The lack of local preparedness to respond to the flood drove home for Ohio government the importance of local preparedness. The state made funding for armory construction available to many communities for their local National Guard Units, of which Defiance had two: Company G and The Sixth Regiment Band. Napoleon's Company F's Armory was built first, opening in December of 1914. The Defiance Democrat reported that Defiance's armory would be a duplicate of Napoleon's and house the gear of the nearly 300 men listed on Defiance's guard rolls. Although our armory front says "1914", it was actually built in the spring of 1915 on land donated by Defiance City Council and with funds largely raised in 1914. Initially, the State of Ohio set aside $10,000 for the proposed building, as promised by Governor Cox when he visited Defiance and spoke to its newly-reorganized Chamber of Commerce a year after the Great Flood. The Defiance Chamber took it upon themselves to make the Armory their first order of business. Local Citizens, the Chamber of Commerce and Defiance's own Congressman T. T. Ansberry all worked for funds and received the extra appropriation of an additional $10,000 from the state to build the much needed structure. The Defiance Chamber of Commerce let the drive to raise an additional $10,000 locally. The Armory gave Defiance the assurance that it was prepared should crises strike again. The structure served as a key gathering place for community dances and other projects. It was an important post for the Federal Troops stationed in Defiance protecting its wartime industrial assets and helping with shelter and provisions for WWI Troops passing through the community.

Post WWII the Armory continued its importance as the headquarters for recruitment of a potential General Motors foundry. A contest for willing workers was held at the Armory as Defiance went head to head with Tiffin, Ohio finally winning the contract for the new and modern General Motors plant that pushed Defiance on ahead as a mid-century leader in the automotive industry for northwest Ohio. The Flood of 1913 marked the end of an era and forced Defiance into the beginning years of the modern world we currently know and understand today; a far different type of community than the one previously independently carved from a wild and murky Great Black Swamp.

CREDITS:

Thank you to Sally Snyder for advice and encouragement.

Thanks to Rich Rozevink for the newspaper clippings that got this idea started.

A huge thank you to Victoria Heilshorn for helping me with photo editing.

Thanks to Diana Bauer for proofing and editing.

Thanks to Barbara Warncke for her Grandpa Kimberly photos.

Thanks to Louie A. Simonis, Chris & Stephanie Mack, Cam Williams, Linda & Phil O'Donnell, Angie & Ryan Soukup, Anne Miller and Jeremy Roehrig my HHOD friends, and Jim Hamilton for reading and cheering me on.

Thanks to Jim Hamilton, Dave Etchie and Jo McCormick and Jeremy Roehrig for access to your postcard collections!

Thanks to John Yeutter at Auraflux Creative for assisting with design and Debe Mesker at the Hubbard Company for assisting with printing.

Thanks to Margaret Proulx for her photography skills and capturing the Flood Poles.

Thanks to my husband, Mark Speiser, who lived with me as I wrote.

Thanks to Ashley Speiser for taking my photo.

Thanks to Rod Brown for photos of 651 Clinton St.

CITATIONS AND BIBLIOGRAPHY

Army Corp of Engineers, U.S. Army Detroit District. The Ohio Department of Natural Resources Division of Water and The Maumee Watershed Conservancy District, 1970.

Beohm, Robert B. c. 1975 "Defiance's Colorful Past" A Presentation of Home Savings and Loan. Booklet.

Bronson, Ed. Bronson Collection. Defiance Public Library, Defiance, Ohio. Photos

City Directory of Defiance, OH 1881 - 1882. Compiled & Arranged by Gleason & Baker, Defiance, OH. White & Blymer, Book & Job Printers 1881.

Crescent-News, (1913, March 27 - 31) Multiple Newspaper Articles

Defiance County Directory, Smith's Directory 1912 - 1913, Edgar Smith Publisher, Dorchester, MA.

Defiance Crescent News, "W. F. Kimberly Dies at Age 58; Rites Monday," January 9, 1937 p. 1

Hello Girls, Signal Corps Photo #21981, Courtesy of National Archives

History of Defiance County Illustrated 1976, Defiance County Historical Society Published 1976 by Taylor Publishing Company, Dallas, TX

https://www2.census.gov/library/publications/decennial/1900/bulletins/demographic/108-mortality-statistics-1909.pdf

https://nationalcalamityeaster1913flood.blogspot.com/2017/03/

https://www.history.com/news/10-things-you-may-not-know-about-the-pinkertons

https://ohiohistorycentral.org/w/Vonderheide_Act

https://www2.census.gov/library/publications/decennial/1900/bulletins/demographic/108-mortality-statistics-1909.pdf

Northwestern Ohio Volunteer Firemen's Association Convention Book, 1906

Panoramic Souvenir of the 1913 Flood in Defiance, Ohio. The Corday & Gross Company, Cleveland.

Paulding Progress, (1913, February 6) Newspaper Article "A Little Touchy"

Slocum, Charles. 1905 "History of the Maumee River Basin". Republished 1982 by Stephen Kryder and reprinted by The Hubbard Company. Last Shiptimber p. 541.

Warner, Beers & Co. (1883). History of Defiance County, OH. Defiance, Ohio: Reprinted by the Defiance County Historical Society.

INTERVIEWS

The Author takes full credit for statements made within this book; but certainly appreciates the guidance and insight the following have provided:

Lynn Lantz
Richard Rozevink
Warren Schlatter
Louis Simonis
Father John Stites
Barbara Warncke

Last Name Spellings in the Book:

Spellings of last names in this publication are taken from the actual primary records, where they may have been misspelled, or the spellings may have changed over the past 100 years to a more Americanized version.

1913 Flood - Blue

1982 Flood - Yellow

2005 Flood - Red

Margaret Proulx photo taken May 20, 2020 at Kingsbury Park.
Flood pole to the right foreground. Blue arrow marks 1913 Flood height.

Some Things Old Are New Again in Defiance, Ohio

The 1871 Scheuerman home was purchased by Paul March for his photography studio (see photo left).

Rod Brown joined Mr. March and became only the third owner, finally selling the studio to Mark & Trish Speiser in 2021 when he and wife, Linda, retired. Photo, right, courtesy of Rod Brown. See Scheuerman Family, below in 1871 era photo.

Available for Gatherings!

The Speisers have converted the building to The Event Studio at 651. Hoping to preserve the building and still share it with the community, the building is being renovated as an event space and available for small gatherings. For more details, visit the website: www.eventstudio651.com.

Photo Restoration!

Artist Victoria Heilshorn has opened a beautiful shoppe downtown, History Studios, retailing unique gifts and books suitable for all ages, complete with an old fashioned candy counter.

Victoria is also an excellent restorer of photos! She cleaned up the photos seen in this book and can work wonders on your photos too! "Vicki" has over ten years of experience restoring, colorizing and editing photos, and she ships! She can also print large, oversized photos for your special occasion. Vicki and Trish are hard at work in the downtown to keep Defiance's rich history alive for generations to come! Watch for more books to come!

The Promise

"Whenever I bring clouds over the earth and the rainbow appears in the clouds, I will remember my covenant between me and you and all living creatures of every kind. Never again will the waters become a flood to destroy all life."

– Genesis 9:14-15